THE **FUTURE** OF **POWER**

HARNESSING
BIOFUELS

NANCY DICKMANN

NEW YORK

Published in 2017 by
The Rosen Publishing Group, Inc.
29 East 21st Street, New York, NY 10010

Cataloging-in-Publication Data

Names: Dickmann, Nancy.
Title: Harnessing biofuels / Nancy Dickmann.
Description: New York : PowerKids Press, 2017. | Series: The future of power | Includes index.
Identifiers: ISBN 9781499432107 (pbk.) | ISBN 9781499432275 (library bound) |
   ISBN 9781508153283 (6 pack)
Subjects: LCSH: Biomass energy--Juvenile literature.
Classification: LCC TP339.D54 2017 | DDC 333.95'39--dc23

For Brown Bear Books Ltd:
Editor: Tim Harris
Editorial Director: Lindsey Lowe
Children's Publisher: Anne O'Daly
Design Manager: Keith Davis
Picture Manager: Sophie Mortimer

Picture Credits: t=top, c=center, b=bottom, l=left, r=right. Interior: 123rf: 22, Borislav Marinic 9br, Jolanta
Rutkowska 13b, Satit Srihin 7, Sukkunta Suppajit 27br, Anastsy Yarmolvich 9t; Alamy: Ashley Cooper 17; Getty
Images: Pedro Ladeira/AFP 25; Green Car Reports: Stephen Edelstein 27t, US Navy/Stephen Edelstein 29t;
NASA: 29br; National Science Foundation: US Government 24; Shutterstock: 6, 10, 13t, 15b, Mykola Ivash-
chenko 5, Naviya Koomprawat 19, Ari Nair 15t, Franshendrick Tambunan 23; Wikipedia: Luiz N. P 20-21.

Manufactured in the United States of America
CPSIA Compliance Information: Batch #BW17PK: For Further Information contact Rosen Publishing, New York, New York at 1-800-237-9932

CONTENTS

FUEL FROM PLANTS

A fuel is anything that can be burned to release energy. We use a lot of different fuels to power our lives. You may have burned charcoal on a barbecue, or used wood to make a campfire. Gasoline (which is made from oil) fuels our vehicles, and natural gas is burned in power stations to generate electricity.

All of these fuels started out as living things. Oil, coal, and natural gas formed from the remains of plants and animals that died millions of years ago. Other fuels, such as wood, formed much more recently when a tree grew in the ground. When we burn wood, we are releasing energy that was stored in the tree.

"Biomass" is the name given to material from living—or recently living—organisms. Fossil fuels are not considered to be biomass because they formed so long ago. Biomass includes wood and crops such as soybeans and corn, as well as animal waste. Some types of biomass—like wood—are used directly, in their natural form. Others are processed to produce liquid fuels called biofuels. Biomass is a form of renewable energy, because we can grow more to replace what we use.

FIRE FOR COOKING

Some scientists believe that early humans used fire to cook their food almost two million years ago.

MILLIONS OF PEOPLE USE FIREWOOD AS A FUEL TO COOK THEIR FOOD. WOOD IS A CHEAP, READILY AVAILABLE BIOFUEL.

HOW PLANTS MAKE FOOD

The energy in plants originally comes from the Sun. Most plants do not eat other organisms, so they must make their own food instead. They do this by a process called photosynthesis. During photosynthesis, a plant takes in water from the soil and a gas called carbon dioxide from the air. The plant uses energy from sunlight to turn the water and carbon dioxide into chemicals called carbohydrates.

The Sun's energy stays stored in the carbohydrates. The plant uses carbohydrates as food to help it stay alive and grow. If we burn the plant after it has died, the burning process turns the carbohydrates back into carbon dioxide and water and releases the energy captured from the Sun.

ETHANOL FUEL

Ethanol is a type of alcohol that can be burned as a fuel. It is made from the carbohydrates found in corn, barley, sugarcane, sugar beet, and some other plants. Ethanol can be used on its own, but it is often mixed with gasoline or diesel fuel and used to power vehicles.

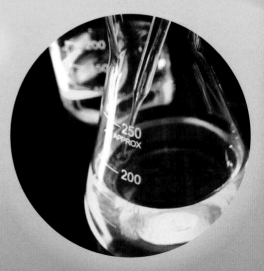

SUGARCANE

After the United States, Brazil is the world's biggest producer of ethanol. Most of Brazil's ethanol comes from its massive sugarcane plantations.

HOW DOES IT WORK?

Using plants for fuel is not a new idea. For well over 100,000 years—and maybe as long ago as two million years—humans have used wood to light fires for cooking and for keeping warm. Early people also burned other types of biomass, such as animal dung and charcoal.

Later, other types of biofuels were used. Thousands of years ago, people around the Mediterranean Sea pressed olives to extract their oil. The oil was used as a fuel for pottery lamps. In other parts of the world, fat from whales and seals was processed to make oil.

People learned to make ethanol, a type of alcohol, from grain. For centuries it was mainly used as a drink, but engineers in the nineteenth century saw its potential as a fuel for machines. Many of the first cars, including the Ford Model T, were designed to run on biofuels.

MODEL T FORD
Henry ford's Model T was the first vehicle to be mass-produced on moving assembly lines. Between 1908–1927, 16.5 million of these cars were built, mostly in Detroit.

RUDOLF DIESEL

Rudolf Diesel was a German engineer who invented the diesel engine to replace the steam engine. Diesel engines could run on vegetable oils, including peanut oil. Many of these engines powered farm machinery. Rudolf Diesel hoped that by using biofuels, farmers would be able to save money by growing their own fuel.

9

BIODIESEL

North America's largest biofuel plant is near Houston, Texas. It converts vegetable oil, animal fat, and grease into a fuel called biodiesel.

MODERN REFINERIES SUCH AS THIS ONE IN EUROPE CONVERT WOOD CHIPS AND OTHER PLANT MATERIAL INTO BIOFUELS.

THE BIOFUEL REVOLUTION

At the same time that cars were becoming more popular, the production of oil and natural gas was increasing. These fossil fuels had already replaced whale oil for lighting, and soon oil replaced biofuels as the most widely used fuel for vehicles. Fossil fuels were cheap, efficient, and practical, so research on biofuels slowed to a halt.

During World War I, there were oil shortages, and ethanol became important again. Even vehicles designed to run on gasoline could use a mixture of gasoline and ethanol to make precious gas supplies go further. In the 1970s there were more oil shortages, and scientists started to look into new ways to make biofuels practical and affordable.

Another reason for the new interest in biofuels is that the fossil fuels we depend on are running out. Biofuels are one of many types of renewable energy that we hope will one day take over from fossil fuels. One big advantage of biomass energy is that it can be made into liquid fuel. Other types of renewable energy, such as wind and solar power, are great for producing electricity, but you can't pump them into a car.

TYPES OF BIOFUELS

There are as many types of biofuels as there are uses for them. Solid biofuels are one of the simplest types. These are fuels that are burned in a solid form, rather than as a liquid. Solid biofuels include wood, sawdust, leaves, animal dung, and even trash. Solid biofuels are sometimes processed before they are burned.

Ethanol, methanol, propanol, and butanol are all types of alcohol biofuels that can be produced from biomass. A natural process called fermentation breaks down the sugars in plants such as corn or sugarcane to make alcohol.

Biodiesel is another kind of biofuel. It is a liquid fuel that is made by refining oils, fats, or greases from plants and animals. It can be made from newly grown crops, such as soybeans or canola. It can even be made from recycled oil collected from restaurants.

Biogas is a gas that is produced when bacteria break down plant and animal matter. It is a mixture of many different gases, including methane, carbon dioxide, and oxygen.

CANOLA

Canola is a kind of rapeseed plant with bright yellow flowers. It is used to make vegetable oil for cooking and biodiesel for powering vehicles.

BIOFUEL BRICKS

Some solid biofuels don't burn very well in their natural states. Sawdust and wood shavings often go through a process called "densifying" to make them easier to burn. They are compressed into small pellets or bricks, and sometimes another substance is added to help it all stick together.

WHEAT STRAW (ABOVE LEFT) IS TURNED INTO PELLETS, WHICH ARE THEN CONVERTED INTO BIOFUELS IN REFINERIES.

BIOFUEL FEEDSTOCKS

Anything that goes into producing biofuels is called a feedstock. There is a huge range of different substances that are used as feedstocks. They include crops, animal fats, animal dung—and even algae and trash!

Plants that are high in starches and sugars make good feedstocks for ethanol and other alcohol-based biofuels. Corn, wheat, sugarcane, and sorghum are all used to make ethanol, and so are a variety of grasses, such as switchgrass.

Substances that contain a lot of oil are good feedstocks for biodiesel. Canola and soybeans are the two most common crops grown for biodiesel, but there are many others, including jatropha and salicornia. Biodiesel can also be made from animal fats that are left over when meat is processed.

ALGAE

One of the most promising feedstocks is algae, which can be used to make several different kinds of biofuels. Algae can be grown in dry or salty places where other crops wouldn't grow. They produce an oil that can be processed into gasoline, diesel, or jet fuel.

FAST FOOD OIL

Biodiesel can be made from used vegetable oil from restaurant kitchens. Many fast food restaurants use hundreds of gallons of vegetable oil a week in their deep fryers. It used to be thrown away after use, but now a lot of it is being filtered and turned into biodiesel.

A COMBINE CUTS WHEAT ON A PRAIRIE. THE WHEAT GRAINS ARE USED TO MAKE FLOUR FOR BREAD. THE STRAW IS USED TO MAKE BIODIESEL.

15

HOW WE USE BIOFUELS

Biofuels have the potential to revolutionize the way we produce energy. This is because they have three main uses: transportation, electricity generation, and heating. Other types of renewable energy, such as hydroelectric power, are really only useful for producing electricity.

Around the world, transportation makes up about 25 percent of our total energy use. Nearly all of this is made up of gasoline and other fossil fuel products. Biofuels such as ethanol and biodiesel can be used to fuel vehicles, and one day they may replace gasoline and diesel.

Even more fuel is used to generate electricity. More than half of the world's electricity is still produced by burning fossil fuels in power plants. However, renewables such as hydroelectric power, wind, solar, and geothermal power are catching up. Gas, liquid, and solid biofuels can all be used to generate electricity, too.

Many people use natural gas to heat their homes, but biofuels can be used too. Pellets made from biomass are an even more practical and efficient way of heating a home.

RECYCLED SODA POP

Soda pop waste is usually sent to wastewater treatment plants. However, technicians have discovered that by adding nitrogen and yeast to the soda pop, it can be used to make ethanol biofuel.

16

FARM WASTE IS LOADED ONTO A TRUCK, WHICH WILL TRANSPORT IT TO A REFINERY TO BE MADE INTO BIOFUEL.

17

GOOD AND BAD

There are a lot of advantages to using biofuels. In fact, many of the things that make fossil fuels so widely used apply to biofuels too. Biofuels are easy to transport, so they can be sent wherever they are needed. They have high energy density, which means that a fairly small amount of fuel will produce a large amount of energy. They can be used in many standard vehicle engines, with only minor modifications needed. And they can be used whenever they are needed, unlike electricity from solar power, which can only be generated when the Sun is shining.

SUSTAINABLE FUELS

There are ways in which biofuels are even more attractive than fossil fuels. Instead of eventually running out, biofuels can be harvested and then grown again each year. They are also biodegradable, which means that if they are accidentally spilled into the environment, they break down naturally. Unlike fossil fuels, which are only found in certain places, biofuel feedstocks can be grown in many locations around the world. They can even be made by recycling substances such as used oil and trash, which would otherwise go to waste.

BIOFUELS POWER MANY CAR ENGINES.
UNLIKE FOSSIL FUELS, BIOFUELS SUCH
AS ETHANOL WILL NOT RUN OUT.

19

ARE BIOFUELS GOOD FOR THE PLANET?

We need to find an alternative to fossil fuels because the world's supply will eventually run out. However, there is another very important reason for using less: burning fossil fuels damages the planet.

Fossil fuels cause air pollution and release carbon dioxide into the atmosphere. When carbon dioxide builds up in the atmosphere, it traps the Sun's heat instead of letting it bounce back into space. This is called the

BUSES IN THE BRAZILIAN CITY OF CURITIBA RUN ON 100 PERCENT BIOFUEL. THEIR EMISSIONS ARE MUCH CLEANER THAN THOSE OF DIESEL BUSES.

greenhouse effect, and it is causing Earth's climate to change in dangerous ways.

Biofuels do produce some pollution, but less than fossil fuels do. They also release carbon dioxide when they are burned. In theory, biofuels should be "carbon neutral." This means that they don't contribute to global warming because the amount of carbon dioxide released when they are burned is the same as the amount the feedstock plants took in when they were alive.

However, farmers use energy for growing the crops: plowing the fields, planting the seeds, and harvesting the plants. Energy is also used when converting the plants to biofuels. This means that in most cases, biofuels produce more carbon dioxide than they take in.

THE END OF FOSSIL FUELS

Oil, natural gas, and coal are fossil fuels. They were formed millions of years ago when dead plants and animals were buried underground, compressed, and became carbon-rich sources of fuel. Eventually, they will run out.

CROPS GROWN FOR BIOFUEL FEEDSTOCK TAKE UP HUGE AREAS OF LAND. SOMETIMES, FORESTS THAT PROVIDE HABITATS FOR RARE ANIMALS ARE CUT DOWN TO MAKE WAY FOR THE CROPS.

SUSTAINABLE BIOFUELS

Biofuels are considered to be a type of renewable energy, but they are only truly renewable when they are managed correctly. A crop of corn used to make ethanol is renewable if the land is replanted with more corn the next year. However, cutting down trees to use their wood releases carbon that may have been stored for hundreds of years. It can take decades for new trees to grow.

In many places, forests are being cleared so that farmers can grow feedstock crops instead. Huge areas of rain forest have been cut down in order to plant palm trees. The fruits of the palm trees can be used to make biodiesel. But logging the forests releases carbon dioxide into the atmosphere. It also destroys important habitats.

ORANGUTANS

Orangutans live in rain forests on the Asian islands of Sumatra and Borneo. Unfortunately, many of these rain forests are being cut down to make space for palm oil plantations. With their habitat destroyed, many orangutans starve to death or are killed by hunters. At least 3,000 orangutans die this way each year.

NOT ENOUGH LAND?

There is only so much land that is suitable for growing crops. If we use some of it for growing biofuel feedstocks, there is less land available to grow food. This is a problem because the world's population is growing, and there are already millions of people who don't have enough to eat.

We simply don't have space to grow enough biofuels to meet the world's needs and still grow enough food. Many farmers want to grow biofuels because they can earn more money than by growing food crops. However, this could make food prices go up.

Growing some types of biofuel feedstocks uses a lot of water, so biofuel production could lead to water shortages. In addition, biofuel crops are often treated with fertilizers. These can cause pollution when they are washed into rivers and streams.

FUNGUS FEEDSTOCK

We need to find new feedstocks that use up less land. Scientists have discovered a fungus that grows on trees in South America. It produces a mixture of chemicals almost identical to diesel fuel. This fungus may become an important feedstock.

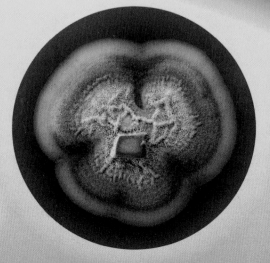

BRAZILIAN CAMPAIGNERS PROTEST AGAINST THE DESTRUCTION OF THE RAIN FORESTS.

THE FUTURE

Many people see biofuels as "transition fuels." This means that they can help plug the gap as the world slowly moves from fossil fuels to renewable energy. At the moment, the world is set up to run on fossil fuels: our power plants, vehicles, and other machines are all designed to use them. It will take a long time to replace all this with electric cars, hydroelectric plants, and wind farms. Although biofuels have their problems, they are still cleaner than fossil fuels. They may be able to power the world while we replace our machines with ones that run on renewable energy.

FUEL FOR CARS

Biofuels currently make up about 2 percent of all fuels used for transportation around the world. Most of the gasoline sold in the United States now contains at least some ethanol, often at least 10 percent. The popular E85 fuel contains 85 percent ethanol and 15 percent gasoline. Scientists predict that by 2050, biofuels could make up one fourth of the world's transportation fuel.

THE FUEL THAT POWERS THE 2016 CHEVROLET VOLT IS 85 PERCENT BIOFUEL (ETHANOL) AND 15 PERCENT FOSSIL FUEL (GASOLINE).

BIOGAS FROM TRASH

Using biofuels may help us solve two problems at once. We are running out of places to dump all the garbage that we produce. The good news is that we can produce energy from this waste by converting some trash into ethanol or biogas.

NAVY SHIPS

More and more machines are starting to run on biofuel mixtures. For example, the United States Navy has a target of drawing 50 percent of its fuel from alternative sources. In 2016 they began fueling several ships using a mixture of petroleum and biofuels made from beef fat. Many modern vehicles can already run on a mixture of biofuels and oil-based fuels. Others are being modified or designed to run on a higher percentage of biofuels.

ELECTRICITY FROM BIOFUELS

Every year people find more uses for biofuels. Some chemists at one university invented a fuel cell that can use cooking oil and sugar and to generate electricity. Fuel cells like this may one day replace batteries in cell phones and computers.

When the price of oil is low, it is much cheaper than biofuels. It can be hard to persuade people to switch to a more expensive fuel, even if it is cleaner. But biofuels should become cheaper as technology improves. One day soon we may be using biofuels for more than just transportation!

BIOFUEL FOR PLANES

History was made in 2008 with the first biofuel test flight by a commercial airline. A Virgin Atlantic jet flew from London in the UK to Amsterdam in the Netherlands with one of its engines using a mix containing 20 percent biofuel. Since then, many other airlines have introduced biofuels to their fuel mixtures.

GLOSSARY

algae: Plantlike, mainly aquatic, life-forms.

biodiesel: A fuel made by refining oil, fat, or grease collected from plants and animals. It is used to fuel engines, either alone or with regular diesel.

carbohydrates: A substance such as a starch or sugar that is rich in energy and made up of carbon, hydrogen, and oxygen.

diesel: A mineral oil (a kind of fossil fuel) used as a fuel in engines.

ethanol: A liquid that can be made from sugarcane, corn, wheat, and other vegetable products. It is used to fuel engines, sometimes alone and sometimes mixed with gasoline.

fossil fuels: Fuels such as coal, oil, and natural gas that are the buried remains of plants and animals that lived long ago.

fuel cell: A device that changes the chemical energy of a fuel into electrical energy.

gasoline: A liquid made from petroleum and used as a fuel for engines.

global warming: An increase in the average temperature of Earth's atmosphere.

habitats: The places where animals or plants naturally live and grow.

pollution: The release of substances that have harmful or toxic effects into the atmosphere, rivers, or ocean.

recycling: To make something new from something that has been used before.

FURTHER INFORMATION

BOOKS

Challoner, Jack. *Energy* (Eyewitness).
NY: Dorling Kindersley, 2012.

Newman, Patricia. *Biofuels*. Ann Arbor,
MI: Cherry Lake, 2013.

Sneideman, Joshua, and Erin Twamley.
*Renewable Energy: Discover the Fuel of the Future
with 20 Projects*. White River Junction,
VT: Nomad Press, 2016.

WEBSITES

Due to the changing nature of Internet links,
PowerKids Press has developed an online list
of websites related to the subject of this book.
This site is updated regularly. Please use this
link to access the list:

www.powerkidslinks.com/tfop/biofuel

INDEX